Sunshine Village

The Magic of Bubbly the Soap

By
Rhea Flynt

Illustrated by
Oksana Matiikiv

© Copyright – Rosa Feygin – 2023

It is not legal to reproduce, duplicate, or transmit any part of this document in either electronic means or printed format. Recording of this publication is strictly prohibited.

Dedication

To my dearest Clara,

In the twinkling stars and the endless sky, in every giggle and every sigh, I see a world full of wonder through your eyes. This book is a story, grown from the joy you bring into my life.

To you, my little bundle of happiness, and to all the children who find delight in the simplest of things – may these tales of animal friends inspire you to dance in the rain of good habits. Let each page turn with the magic of washing hands, brushing teeth, and all the little things that make you shine bright. With every story, remember how much you're loved, for you are the sparkle in the stars and the laughter in the wind.

Forever by your side,

Acknowledgments

My deepest gratitude goes to my entire family, whose collective love, creativity, and passion have been the pulsing heart of "In Sunshine Village."
And to Clara, my granddaughter, your childlike wonder and infectious joy have been a vivid reminder of the magic and curiosity that life holds. Your laughter and bright eyes have brought the characters of Sunshine Village to life.

To all my readers, I hope this story resonates with the warmth of family and the simple joys that enrich our lives. May it bring smiles to your faces.

With heartfelt thanks and appreciation,

Rhea Flynt

About the Author

As a child growing up in the vibrant city of St. Petersburg, Russia, my life was always filled with the melodies of music and the rhythms of learning. My early years were spent in the halls of a musical pedagogical college, where I not only honed my musical skills but also delved deep into the world of psychology and education. Those years were magical, surrounded by notes and theories, learning how music can touch souls and open young minds to a world of possibilities.

After my formal training, I found myself drawn to the joyous task of teaching music to young children. Each day was a new song, a fresh start to instill in them a love for melody and rhythm. But as life often plays its own tunes, my journey took an unexpected turn, leading me across the world to the United States. Here, I ventured into the realm of Information Technology, intrigued by its potential to connect and create.

Despite the shift in my career, one thing remained constant – my understanding and love for children's emotions and development. My background in psychology and education, coupled with my musical roots, always kept me close to the world of childhood wonder and learning.

Now, I am embarking on a new adventure, one that harmonizes my past with my present. As a writer of children's books, I aim to bring joy and learning to little ones through playful stories and charming characters.

Through my stories, I hope to spread love, laughter, and learning to children everywhere, encouraging them to explore, imagine, and grow. Because in the end, it's all about making each note of life count, one story at a time.

In Sunshine Village, which you might not have heard about at all,
Lived furry friends, loved by all.
Benny the bear and Sally the squirrel,
With Robbie the rabbit, they'd dance and twirl.

But one day, trouble came down,
A sickness spread, and spirits went down.
Grandpa Owl couldn't find a cure,
How to solve this mystery, they weren't sure.

Then magic appeared, as Bubbly the Soap,
Bringing hope and a way to cope.
"I've got a secret," Bubbly said,
"To help your friends, tucked in bed."

Benny, Sally, and Robbie were keen,
To learn the secret, to help them stay clean.
"Wash your hands, it's simple and true,
With soap and water, a scrub will do!"

Before you eat and after play,
Wash those germs and dirt away.
When hands are dirty or after a sneeze,
Washing often puts minds at ease.

Always wash them before each meal,
And after playing, that's the deal.
When you cough or touch your nose,
Wash your hands; it's what Bubbly shows.

The friends were puzzled but gave it a whirl,
Benny, Sally, and Robbie, each boy and girl.
They washed their hands, scrubbed them just right,
And soon enough, their hearts were light.

The village healed, the animals cheered,
Following Bubbly's advice, the sickness was cleared.
Now Benny, Sally, and Robbie knew,
The secret of handwashing, and you do too!

So always remember, before you eat,
Or play with friends, please be so sweet,
To wash your hands, keep them clean,
And you'll stay healthy, like a sunbeam's gleam!

www.ingramcontent.com/pod-product-compliance
Lightning Source LLC
Chambersburg PA
CBHW041215240426
43661CB00012B/1053